duck YEAH!
An Illustrated Story For Adults On Willpower

PETE WILLIAMS

When morning dawns and you rise

three ducks will help you win the prize.

To guarantee your day is great

it can't be left to luck or fate.

You have to prioritise the day,

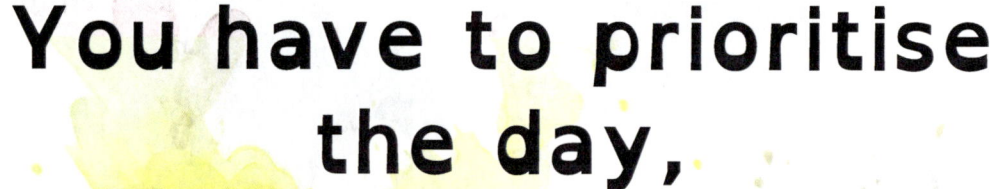

to make sure it will go your way.

Your three ducks are made of willpower

but they'll vanish at the 24th hour.

You only have three ducks to give,

so be careful what stuff you use them with.

Choose your goals, don't count on luck.

Work hard and really 'give a duck'.

Willpower helps
with many things,

but you only get
three ducklings.

To reach your goals,
there's no secret key.

Just hard work
with those ducks...

Use 'em early
and you'll likely crash.

But use 'em wisely and today you'll smash.

So how will you use them to make it great?

So keep your cool above the surface.

Beneath the water, just stay on purpose.

Because at the end, you'll shout with glee,

A Duck is A Terrible Thing To Waste
- A Short Fowl-Mouthed Essay -

As we've learned from our feathered friends, willpower is valuable and limited.

So, how can we better manage our daily challenges, craft a happier life, and make the most of our precious ducks?

First, we must understand that...

A "shit" is a unit of measurement that measures effort-events. A shit could be something that happens to you, as well as things that could, should, or need to happen.

Some effort-events are important *(important shit)*, while others are unimportant (regular *shit*).

We say effort-events because not all shits are "tasks".

Most people have a lot of *shit to do*, but they also *think about shit*, and get *distracted by shit*. Sometimes, *shit comes at us from nowhere*. Other times *we bring shit upon ourselves*.

"Fucks" are a unit of measurement too.

A fuck is one unit of willpower, effort, or attention (focused or unfocused).

Fucks are the currency you use to *get shit done*, or to *think about shit*.

The key difference between a shit and a fuck is that shit is external to us, while fucks are within us.

Shit happens.

Sometimes people *give us shit to do*.
Sometimes they just *give us the shits*.

We can't always control the shit in our lives, but we can choose whether we *give a fuck about it*.

Remember: You can't give a fuck about everything!

Have you ever heard about Christine Miserandino's spoon theory? It's a metaphor for understanding limited energy reserves, particularly for people with chronic illnesses or disabilities. In this context, spoons represent units of energy or resources available to an individual each day.

Similar to the spoon theory, you only have a limited number (we estimate 3–7) of fucks to give per day. But there is always more shit you could be giving a fuck about than you have fucks to give.

Managing your fucks involves carefully allocating them, prioritising tasks, and making difficult choices about how to spend your limited energy — whatever you call it — willpower, spoons, or ducks.

If you try to fill the day with too much shit, you'll run out of fucks before you run out of day

...and then you'll feel bad that you didn't *get enough shit done.*

Feeling bad is just more shit to worry about. If you spend too much time giving a fuck, you'll have even fewer fucks to give to more important shit.

This is not sustainable. In fact, it's a fucking downward spiral.

It's far better to budget your fucks by scheduling less shit

...and leaving some left over at the end of the day.

Plus, *urgent shit* will come up from time to time, so, it's handy to have a few surplus fucks in your pocket each day.

By being mindful of your willpower reserves (fucks), you can better navigate your daily challenges (the shit), and maintain a more sustainable and enjoyable life

— *that's truly worth giving a duck about!*

© 2024 Pete Williams
Published by Preneur Press
www.duckyeah.life

The moral right of the author has been asserted.

For quantity sales or media enquiries, please contact the publisher at the website address above.

A catalogue record for this book is available from the National Library of Australia

ISBN: 978-0-6483167-1-8 (hardback)
978-0-6483167-2-5 (paperback)

Cover Design and Interior Layout by Studio 1 Design
Publishing Consultant Linda Diggle

All rights reserved. Except as permitted under the Australian Copyright Act 1968 (for example, a fair dealing for the purposes of study, research, criticism or review), no part of this book may be reproduced, stored in a retrieval system, communicated or transmitted in any form or by means without written permission. All inquiries should be made to the publisher at the above address.

Disclaimer: Although the author and publisher have made every effort to ensure the information in this book was correct at press time, the author and publisher do not assume and hereby disclaim any liability to any party for any loss, damage, or disruption caused by errors or omissions, whether such errors or omissions result from negligence, accident, or any other cause.

www.ingramcontent.com/pod-product-compliance
Lightning Source LLC
Chambersburg PA
CBRC092341290426
44109CB00009B/180